The Way It Was — PART 2

Published by Momentum Books, L.L.C., a subsidiary of Hour Media, L.L.C.

117 West Third Street
Royal Oak, Michigan 48067
momentumbooks.com

COPYRIGHT © 2011 BY HOUR MEDIA, L.L.C.

Printed and bound in China

FIRST EDITION: September 2011

ISBN: 978-1-879094-92-5
LCCN: 2011932521

The Way It Was —❧— PART 2

MORE GLIMPSES OF DETROIT'S HISTORY
FROM THE PAGES OF *HOUR DETROIT* MAGAZINE

MOMENTUM BOOKS, L.L.C.
ROYAL OAK, MICHIGAN

GEORGE BULANDA

Introduction

SOMETIMES HITTING THE REWIND BUTTON IS A WONDROUS THING, MORE UPLIFTING THAN A ZOLOFT pill or a stiff drink — and without any side effects. The past is comforting because we know exactly what to expect. The present and the future are put on pause, and we can revel in the consoling embrace of the past.

Nostalgia is an anodyne, a device to dull the pain and discomfort of the present — or the prospects of a frightening future. That's why we look at scrapbooks, attend school reunions, read old love letters, reminisce with family and friends — and bask in happy memories of a bold and bright city.

In that spirit, this volume should be considered a scrapbook of Detroit, one covering 111 years, from an 1869 image of the original Detroit Opera House on Campus Martius to a 1980 photograph of Ronald and Nancy Reagan on the podium at Joe Louis Arena during the Republican National Convention.

Just as with the first *The Way It Was* book, published in 2004, there is no particular order, structure, or timeline in *The Way It Was, Part 2,* just a collection of photos that chronicle Detroit as it was through more than a century. It is by no means comprehensive, nor does it aspire to be. Neither is it a formal historical chronicle of the city. However, it does offer a potent portrait of a time long vanished.

There are famous people — George Washington Carver, Joe Louis (two pictures, in fact, a happenstance he shares with Benson Ford Sr.), Carol Channing, George Romney, Hank Greenberg, The Supremes, Charles Lindbergh, Henry Ford II, Ed Asner, Berry Gordy Jr., Presidents Eisenhower and Reagan, even Mayor Coleman Young dressed as Santa Claus. But there are also images of "ordinary" Detroiters lined up for a movie at the Madison Theatre; young people congregating in front of the Grande Ballroom; kids taking a summertime dip at Water Works Park; boys playing a game of street shinny; a crowd packing Woodward for a glimpse of Santa in front of Hudson's; well-dressed folks attending the Metropolitan Opera's tour at Masonic Temple; worshippers at Shaarey Zedek and St. Florian; Christmas shoppers jamming Kern's; children on the playground at the Brewster-Douglass Projects; a truckload of people downtown celebrating the end of World War II.

Almost without exception, the pictures capture happy memories.

"No one ever takes a photograph of something they want to forget," actor Robin Williams says in the 2002 film *One Hour Photo*. Williams plays a disturbed man who works in the photo-development department of a Wal-Mart like store, a grim emporium bathed in fluorescent light and stocked with tacky merchandise. A pathetically lonely man, he fills his off-work hours fantasizing about the exciting, full lives he sees in the photos he develops. It's a harmless enough pursuit, until his fantasies turn deadly.

Williams may have played a loony character, but what he said has merit, for the pictures we decide to shoot, the ones we treasure most, are invariably from joyous times: birthdays, anniversaries, bar mitzvahs, a girlfriend or boyfriend in the early flush of love, a family reunion, a European vacation, a first apartment. We freeze that moment in the split second of a camera click, a futile but altogether human effort to preserve a moment forever. Lives change, people die, circumstances are altered, but those memories remain as vivid as the moment in which they were lived.

I was reminded of that line from *One Hour Photo* when I thought back to interviewers' questions when the first *The Way It Was* book was published. "Why are just good times shown?" "Why are there no photos of strife?" they inquired.

I explained that the book, just like the new edition you're holding, is like a scrapbook or family album, and unless you're a member of the Addams family, ghastly memories aren't included.

Also, in a city as tarnished as Detroit is, do we want to add another blemish to an already scarred visage? Does anyone really need to see another photo of the decaying Michigan Central Depot? Another trite image of an empty building defaced by graffiti? Boarded-up homes in unsafe neighborhoods? Do we want to see graphic images of fires, riots, demolitions, criminal activity?

No, we want to remember and treasure the good times. The trouble is, memory lane goes in only one direction — backward. Eventually, we have to get back on the track of the present.

But for now, indulge yourself in the soft, twilit glow of nostalgia. *The Way It Was II, Part 2* is a ticket back to an era when the city throbbed with vitality.

All aboard! — *George Bulanda*

**1869** THE TALL BUILDING BEYOND THE FOUNTAIN ON CAMPUS MARTIUS IS THE spanking-new Detroit Opera House, which opened on March 29, 1869. Despite its name, the venue offered all sorts of entertainment. The grand opening, in fact, featured a musical comedy with Kate Reignolds, a leading comedienne of the day. Later that year, Detroit was treated to its first symphonic concert at the hall, and, in 1914, the Detroit Symphony Orchestra played its premiere concert there. The interior was decorated by Detroit artist Robert Hopkin, including the main curtain, which was painted by Hopkin and bore the inscription: "So fleet the works of men, back to their earth again. Ancient and holy things fade like a dream." The Detroit Opera House itself faded after a fire in 1897, but it was quickly rebuilt. In the 1920s, it became the Shubert Detroit Opera House. Originally, the main floor was dedicated to retail, and in this photo, the Newcomb-Endicott & Co. store occupied the space. In 1881, J.L. Hudson opened a men's clothing shop there, which eventually relocated and grew into Hudson's department store. In the '30s, the auditorium was gutted, and Sam's Discount Department Store set up shop until the block was demolished in 1966.

—❧—

1905

IN ITS HEYDAY, BELLE ISLE OFFERED MANY AMENITIES, BUT A TRIP TO THE ISLAND wasn't complete without a visit to the aquarium. Designed by Albert Kahn, the Belle Isle Aquarium opened to the public on Aug. 18, 1904. Although the structure's ornamental façade was attractive, its interior was even more alluring. The vaulted ceiling and walls were covered in green tiles, lending the effect of being under water. Eventually, attendance waned, particularly after the closure of the Belle Isle Zoo. In 2005, the city, faced with a crushing $230 million deficit, announced plans to shutter the aquarium. A group called Friends of the Belle Isle Aquarium (FOBIA) scrambled to save what was then the oldest operating aquarium in the country. But it was to no avail; the city closed the building on April 3, 2005, and the marine creatures were moved to other aquariums and zoos. In 2011, FOBIA President Vance Patrick said the group was still committed to reopening the aquarium, which continues to be maintained.

 BORN IN GRAND RAPIDS IN 1876, ROBERT CRAIG HUPP WAS A GEARHEAD LONG before the word was coined. In 1887, his family moved to Detroit, and soon afterward the burgeoning auto industry fascinated Hupp. After working with Olds, Ford, and Regal, he started his own auto company in 1909. Hupp wanted to create an affordable car for the masses, and the idea clicked. The first Hupmobile (only one "p" was used in the car's name) was introduced at the Detroit Automobile Show in 1909. Priced at $750, the Model 20 was a sales hit. But internal squabbles at the Hupp Motor Car Co. forced R.C. Hupp to leave the firm in 1911, the same year this photo of a Hupmobile was captured on Lafayette in downtown Detroit. In that year, 6,079 Hupmobiles were sold, according to *The Standard Catalog of American Cars*. But 1928 was the company's best year, when almost 66,000 were snapped up. By then, the Hupmobile was renowned for its styling and more powerful engine; the original four-cylinder was just a memory. Hupp joined other auto ventures, but they all fizzled. Still, Hupp remained active in the industry, becoming a major force with the Four Wheel Hydraulic Brake Co. After playing a game of squash at the Detroit Athletic Club in 1931, Hupp died of a massive cerebral hemorrhage in the locker room. He was 55. The company bearing his name didn't hang on much longer. In 1940, the firm's last year, only 319 autos were produced.

 THE PICTURE OF THESE MEN WATCHING A BASEBALL GAME SEEMS INNOCUOUS enough, but it masks a dishonorable reality. These spectators at Navin Field (later Briggs Stadium, then Tiger Stadium) are seated in the segregated section of the ballpark. In those days, there were also no African-Americans who played for the Tigers. It wasn't until 1958 that the team was integrated with the arrival of infielder Ozzie Virgil, more than a decade after Brooklyn Dodger Jackie Robinson broke through the color line in 1947. But back in the early decades of the last century, black ballplayers were active in the Negro National League. The Detroit Stars, part of the NNL, played at Mack Park, at Mack and Fairview, from 1920-1929, and then after it burned down, at Hamtramck Stadium for a couple of years, until the group disbanded. Perhaps the best known of the Stars was slugger Norman "Turkey" Stearnes, who picked up a slew of home-run titles. A second Negro National League was formed in 1933, and the Negro American League came along in 1937.

1913 A<small>DULTS OFTEN UNDERESTIMATE THE CREATIVE CAPACITY OF CHILDREN, WHO CAN BE</small> just as inventive as their elders, if not more so. At play, young people are wonderfully adept at improvising. That appears to be the case in this circa-1913 photo, which shows a group of boys on an unidentified Detroit street engaged in shinny, a kind of poor man's hockey that's played on ice, turf, or the street. There are few rules, and equipment is extemporaneous. Sticks can be improvised from broom handles or tree branches; a ball, tin can, or chunk of ice may substitute for a puck; and goals might be constructed from rocks or garbage cans. The word "shinny" is likely a corruption of the Scottish game shinty, which is especially popular in the Highlands. Although automobiles were quickly replacing horses at the time of this picture, the man in the background seems content using the old mode of transportation.

1915 SINCE 1927, DETROIT'S REPOSITORY OF GREAT ART HAS BEEN HOUSED IN THE sprawling Paul Cret-designed Italian Renaissance building on Woodward. But before there was a Detroit Institute of Arts (DIA), there was the Detroit Museum of Art, an imposing Romanesque-style structure designed by James Balfour, at East Jefferson and Hastings. The castle-like building, seen here around 1915, opened in 1888. Although an art school and wings were added, the building still proved too small for Detroit's growing population and its concomitant interest in art. When the new DIA opened, the once-lofty Museum of Art served as offices for the Veterans of Foreign Wars. Later, the Public Welfare Department called it home. Finally, the grand old edifice came tumbling down in 1960 to make way for I-75.

1917 Black American soldiers have served valiantly throughout our country's history, but the shameful specter of segregation hovered over them. In addition, African-Americans in the military often were given the most dangerous jobs, or relegated to supply duties. Nonetheless, black soldiers remained patriotic, fighting like wildcats in the Great War. One National Guard unit, the 369th Infantry Regiment (nicknamed the Harlem Hellfighters) were the first Americans — white or black — to reach the combat zone in France and engaged in continuous battle longer than any American unit. It was also the first regiment to reach the Rhine, in 1918. One of the Hellfighters, Sgt. Henry Johnson, was the first American to be decorated with the Croix de Guerre. This photo shows African-American soldiers training at Fort Wayne. The white soldiers in the foreground are probably officers. Although World War I began in 1914, the U.S. didn't declare war on Germany until 1917. Retired Chief Curator James Conway confirmed that this building is Barracks 314, which still stands today, although Conway said the two-story porch is gone. It wasn't until after World War II that President Harry Truman desegregated the armed forces.

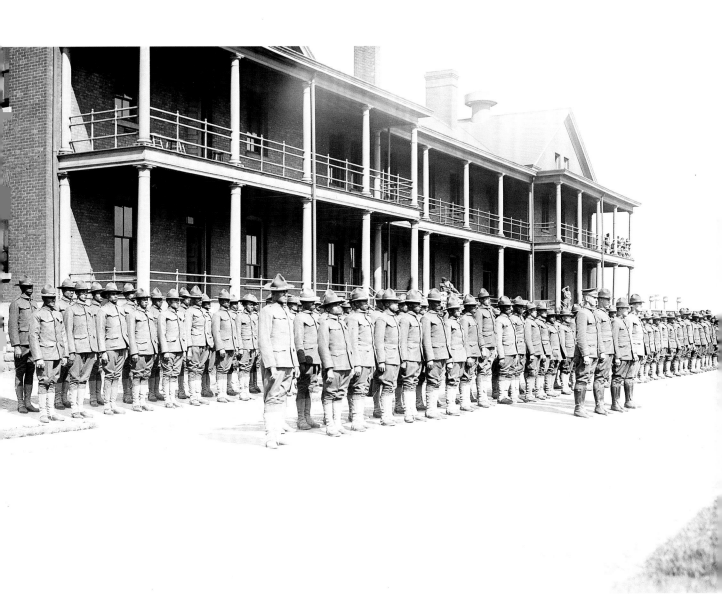

⟡

1917

Detroit has had some grand hotels through the years, including the Book-Cadillac, Fort Shelby, and Statler. But before those were built, the imposing Pontchartrain Hotel, which stood where the First National Building on Woodward is today, was a posh place for visitors to stay, along with the Hotel Tuller. Many Detroiters also enjoyed social events in the Pontchartrain's opulent meeting places, such as the Flamingo Room. The 10-story hotel (five stories were added in 1916) opened on Oct. 29, 1907, on Cadillac Square and Woodward. At left is the Soldiers and Sailors Monument, commemorating Michigan's servicemen who died in the Civil War. The Pontchartrain's time in the sun was brief. When the Statler Hotel opened in 1915, it boasted 800 rooms — twice as many as the Pontchartrain — each with its own private bath. In those days, it was common for hotel guests to have to use public restrooms and baths down the hall. Only some of the Pontchartrain's rooms had private baths. Then the tony Fort Shelby on Lafayette opened in 1916. The outdated Pontchartrain couldn't compete, and in 1920 it was razed. Years later, in 1965, another hotel bearing the Pontchartrain name was built in downtown Detroit on Washington Boulevard, across from Cobo Hall.

1919

MANY DETROITERS WILL RECOGNIZE THIS NEOCLASSICAL BUILDING AT WOODWARD and Eliot as Wayne State University's Bonstelle Theatre. But before its theatrical incarnation, it was the new home of Temple Beth El, designed by Detroit architect and Temple Beth El member Albert Kahn, in 1902. According to Irwin J. Cohen's *Jewish Detroit*, it served the congregation until 1922, when a new structure was built at Woodward and Gladstone. Architect C. Howard Crane, responsible for Detroit's Orchestra Hall and the Fox and Adams theaters, redesigned the building's interior. Actress, drama coach, and theater company manager Jessie Bonstelle, known as "the maker of stars," staged performances at the new 1,200-seat Bonstelle Playhouse. Briefly, it was also known as the Detroit Civic Theatre. After Bonstelle's death in 1932, the building reopened as the Mayfair, which showed first-run movies. Beginning in 1951, it was used by Wayne State University's theater department and continues to be the venue for the department's undergraduate program. As Wayne State students, Lily Tomlin, Tom Sizemore, and Tom Skerritt — who all went on to national acclaim — performed on the Bonstelle's stage. There's an added element to the building's lore. It's said that the ghost of Jessie Bonstelle occasionally roams the theater. As for Temple Beth El, it thrives today on Telegraph near 14 Mile, its home since 1974.

**AT FIRST GLANCE, THIS BUSTLING STREET SCENE WITH A DOUBLE-DECKER BUS** might be mistaken for London. But in the 1920s, such buses were a common sight on Detroit's busiest thoroughfares. This circa-1921 photo shows a traffic-choked Grand Boulevard and Second (notice the traffic cop and the old-fashioned signal at lower right). The Detroit Motorbus Co. unveiled a fleet of two-tiered buses; the first ran down Jefferson in 1920, and other routes were soon added. Originally, the buses had open tops, such as the one in this photo. The bare trees and heavily garbed passengers pictured here suggest that the season is either late autumn or winter, making for a brisk commute. Later models had covered top tiers. Double-deckers were so popular that the rival Detroit Street Railway (DSR) added 50 gas-electric buses to the city's most-traveled lines in 1926-27. By the end of 1931, the Detroit Motorbus Co. was taken over by the city-run DSR.

⁓

1923   IF YOU DOUBT THAT METRO DETROITERS ARE "THE SALT OF THE EARTH," JUST LOOK down — about 1,200 feet. In the city's cellar are more than 1,400 acres of salt mines, remnants of what was a sea millions of years ago. The men wearing headlamps here are using pickaxes to hack at salt rocks. The mineshaft's opening is on Sanders Street on the west side of Detroit, and the maze runs beneath Dearborn's Rouge complex, Melvindale, and Allen Park. Opened in 1896, the mine was operated for years by the International Salt Mine Co. until 1983, when it closed. But the mine reopened in 1997, when the Detroit Salt Co. assumed ownership, supplying Michigan and other states with rock salt to melt hazardous ice on winter roadways. In 1940, Detroit became the first major city to use rock salt to control snow and ice.

❧

1925 SOMETIMES IT SEEMS THAT KIDS ARE SMARTER THAN ADULTS. GROWN-UPS COMPLAIN endlessly about the snow — driving in it, shoveling it, even looking at it. The kvetching seems only to prolong the winter, and there's not a blessed thing anyone can do about the snow and cold anyway. Young folks, on the other hand, have the right idea. Instead of whining about winter, they join forces with it, exulting in tobogganing, sledding, skating, making snow angels and snowmen, or maybe engaging in a playful snowball fight. And there's always the hope of a school-free snow day to enjoy. These boys, decked out in 1920s-style knickers and caps on an undisclosed Detroit street, appear to be having a blast rolling a giant snowball, perhaps to make a gargantuan snowman. When winter rolls around, it's probably best to take a leaf from the kids in this picture and make the best of it.

DRIVERS ALONG NORTHWESTERN HIGHWAY IN SOUTHFIELD CAN'T MISS Congregation Shaarey Zedek, with its concrete-and-stained-glass apex jutting dramatically heavenward. The name translates to "gates of righteousness" or "gates of justice" from the Hebrew. Built in 1962 by Percival Goodman, the synagogue is an architectural marvel of mid-century style. But it's only the latest of seven buildings for Detroit's oldest Conservative Jewish congregation, which began in 1861. Its first building was at Congress and St. Antoine, in downtown Detroit. Other locations followed, including this neoclassical- and Romanesque-influenced building at Willis and Brush. At the time of this circa-1925 photo, just a few more years remained before another move, to temporary quarters in 1930, and then to Chicago Boulevard and Lawton, which would be Shaarey's Zedek's home from 1932-62. In a sense, there are actually eight buildings in the congregation's history. In the early '90s, a merger with B'nai Israel created the Shaarey Zedek B'nai Israel Center in West Bloomfield Township.

━━━⟨∾⟩━━━

1926
WINDOW SHOPPING MAY HAVE GONE THE WAY OF THE BUGGY WHIP, BUT IN the days when Detroiters used to shop downtown instead of at malls, window displays were vital in piquing the interest of customers — and perhaps enticing them to buy. The flagship Hudson's store alone had 51 display windows, all lavishly decorated and tailored to the season. At Christmastime, department-store windows were particularly extravagant, such as this one of dolls and dollhouses, which also includes a painted background. The store in this circa mid-'20s photo is unknown, but its holiday presentation certainly succeeded in hooking the attention of these bundled-up children, who appear mesmerized by the toys. In our age, when children yearn for iPods, laptops, designer clothes, cell phones, digital cameras, and other pricey goods, it's sobering to realize that there was once a time when little girls were enraptured by something as simple as a doll.

**1927** DURING THE SCORCHING DOG DAYS OF SUMMER, NOTHING IS MORE BRACING THAN a dip in the pool — or, in the case of these youngsters, a dip in the fountain. In this circa-1927 shot, kids cavort in the Merrill Fountain at Palmer Park, on the city's north side, as adults look on. The fountain, named after lumber baron Charles Merrill, was dedicated in 1901 at its original downtown location on Campus Martius. In 1926, it was moved to its current site near Six Mile and Woodward, in Palmer Park. Speaking at the 1901 dedication was Merrill's son-in-law, former Sen. Thomas Palmer, after whom the park is named. He owned the property, and in the late 19th century, donated it to the City of Detroit, stipulating that it was to be used for a park. Palmer's wife, Elizabeth "Lizzie" Merrill Palmer, bequeathed $3 million in 1916 to found the Merrill-Palmer School for Motherhood and Home Training. Now known as the Merrill-Palmer Skillman Institute, it is affiliated with Wayne State University and is renowned for its research on child and family development.

 WINTER MAY HAVE ITS DRAWBACKS, BUT NEARLY EVERYONE CAN AGREE THAT A blanket of glittering snow brightens a dreary urban landscape. The ethereal beauty of a snowfall is captured here in the late 1920s in Grand Circus Park. As one looks north, the spire of the Central United Methodist Church towers over the park. At rear right stands the now-razed Hotel Wolverine. In the right foreground is a statue of William Cotter Maybury, mayor of Detroit from 1897-1904. Unveiled in 1912, the bronze, marble, and granite monument was created by Adolph Alexander Weinman. The pro-business, conservative Maybury died in 1909. Curiously, across the street on the west side of Woodward is a 1904 statue of Detroit's great reformer mayor and Maybury's political opponent, Hazen S. Pingree, who preceded Maybury in office. The statues were moved in 1997 directly across from each other at the northern entrance of the park, where they eye each other suspiciously in stony silence.

1927 Detroit was flying high in 1927, thanks to its native son, Charles Lindbergh, pictured with his mother at a parade here in his honor. The occasion, of course, was Lucky Lindy's flight from New York to Paris in May of that year in *The Spirit of St. Louis*, becoming the first person to fly solo across the Atlantic and completing his 3,600-mile trip in 33 and a half hours. Ticker-tape parades were also held in New York and St. Louis, Lindbergh was named *Time* magazine's Man of the Year in '27, and President Calvin Coolidge awarded him the Medal of Honor. Lindbergh was born in 1902 at his great-Uncle Edwin's Queen Anne-style home on West Forest (now demolished) near what is now Wayne State University. Although he was brought up primarily in Minnesota, Lindbergh spent many boyhood summers in Detroit with relatives. During World War II, he moved to Bloomfield Hills and worked at the Willow Run bomber plant. His mother, Evangeline, relocated to the city in the early '20s and taught science at Cass Technical High School. And another great-uncle, John C. Lodge, served as mayor of Detroit and has an expressway named after him.

1928

As Detroit spread and prospered during the booming 1920s, its need for more houses of worship grew, too. In Hamtramck, then a predominantly Polish-Catholic enclave, St. Florian Church, founded in 1908, became too small to accommodate the burgeoning parish. In 1928, a Gothic-style church on Poland Street was erected, towering above the simple frame houses in the blue-collar neighborhood. Parishioners, most of whom were factory workers, scraped up their savings to build a new, much larger church. Typical of so many houses of worship in immigrant communities, it dwarfed everything around it, its 200-foot-high steeple jutting heavenward. The building's architectural details are notable on many counts, including the great rose window, and the stained-glass windows in the sanctuary, all representing a Polish saint. Construction began in 1926 and was completed in 1928. This image shows the dedication on Oct. 21, 1928. The edifice was designed by Ralph Adams Cram, who won the American Architect Award for it in 1929. St. Florian was once the second-largest parish in metro Detroit, but like so many churches and schools in aging neighborhoods, its congregation shrank, forcing the closure first of the high school and then the grade school. Detroit City Councilman Kenneth Cockrel Jr. is a 1983 grad. However, the church remains open and, although the worshippers are more diverse than they were in the '20s, St. Florian (who is the patron saint of firefighters) continues to offer Masses in both Polish and English.

1929

The night lends a distinctly dramatic air to a city's skyline, with massive hulks of skyscrapers, dotted with scintillating lights, chiseled against the sable sky. The bright starburst, shining like an otherworldly beacon, crowns what was then the Union Trust Building, which later became known as the Guardian Building. Even the blazing red ball atop the Penobscot Building (right) dims in comparison. The elaborate Art Deco Union Trust edifice, designed by Wirt Rowland, earned the sobriquet "The Cathedral of Finance." When it opened in the heart of downtown on Griswold in 1929, the Guardian was the city's second-tallest building. The Union Trust Co. was founded in 1890 by Col. Frank Hecker, whose magnificent chateau-style home still stands today at Woodward and East Ferry. His business partners included Russell Alger, Dexter Ferry, C.H. Buhl, and Sen. James McMillan. During the booming '20s, the Union Trust was the city's largest bank and was known for assisting common laborers in buying homes. For security reasons — and to conserve energy — illuminations such as the Guardian's were discouraged during World War II. The fear was that enemy planes could more easily bomb targets. Its starburst summit is long gone, but the tangerine-colored Guardian remains one of Detroit's brightest architectural lights.

1929

For many people, childhood Christmas memories are inextricably tied to places in metro Detroit. Some have recollections of the magical Toytown on the 12th floor of the downtown Hudson's department store that can never be erased. Others will forever cherish the holiday displays at Cobo Hall or the Ford Rotunda in Dearborn. Still others will recall Detroit Aglow — the night kicking off the holiday season when downtown buildings, festooned with lights, wreaths, garlands, and other decorations, twinkled like an oversize Christmas village. For the tykes pictured opposite, the memory of a visit from Santa Claus in his sleigh undoubtedly stayed with them throughout their lives. Shot on a snowy Christmas Day in 1929, this photo captures the thrill of kids receiving gifts from St. Nick at an undisclosed Detroit location. And, although a horse is pulling the sleigh instead of Rudolph and his pals, these children hardly seem concerned with the anomaly.

⟨ ❧ ⟩

1931

HERE'S THE ELEGANT EASTOWN THEATRE GETTING READY FOR ITS CLOSE-UP. Workers are busy spiffing up the marquee, while another stands on the building's apex festooning colorful flags for the theater's premiere film, *Sporting Blood*, starring Clark Gable. The Eastown, at Harper and Van Dyke on the city's east side, seated 2,500, and even included a ballroom. Although it was used primarily as a movie theater in its early days, there were occasional stage shows as well. Typical of movie palaces from that era, the décor is a mixture of styles, although the Renaissance Revival motif predominates. After years of decline, the Eastown closed in the mid-'6os, but was revived in May 1969 as a rock 'n' roll venue. Baby boomers will recall seeing such top acts as Traffic, King Crimson, Pink Floyd, Alice Cooper, Emerson, Lake & Palmer, the MC5, Joe Cocker, John Mayall, and Eric Burdon & War. In December 1971, Mayor Roman Gribbs shuttered the theater — which had a reputation as a drug haven — for failing to meet health and safety codes. It reopened briefly in the summer of 1973. In subsequent years, it became a jazz spot. In the early '8os, the Eastown's name was changed to the Showcase. Later that decade, the name was changed back to the Eastown, and plays and musicals were mounted. Techno fans flocked to the theater for raves during the 1990s. Finally, a church moved in. But the Eastown's glory days, as Clark Gable might have said, are gone with the wind. A fire in the adjoining apartments in 2010 spelled the end of the theater. At press time, it was scheduled for demolition.

1931 WE TEND TO THINK OF SUBURBS AS A POST-WORLD WAR II PHENOMENON, BUT some, such as Grosse Pointe, Birmingham, Royal Oak, Wyandotte, and Dearborn, have histories that reach back many years. In the days when train travel reigned supreme, Birmingham was an important hub between Detroit and Pontiac. In fact, according to Craig Jolly's book *Birmingham*, the city's rail service started in 1838. The scene here, photographed on July 15, 1931, shows people either greeting passengers or ready to board the train themselves at the brand-new Grand Trunk Railroad Station, a Tudor Revival-style edifice on South Eton that was built as a reduced version of the train station in Birmingham, England. It replaced a smaller building on Woodward. The station, constructed for $125,000 by Albert H. Aldinger and George B. Walbridge, was vacated in 1978 and, the next year, became a restaurant, Norman's Eton Street Station. Today, it's the site of the Big Rock Chop House. Since 1985, it's been on the roster of the National Register of Historic Places.

1933

EVEN IN THE THICK OF THE DEPRESSION, WHICH SLAMMED DETROIT PARTICULARLY hard, city residents weren't about to allow the grim economy to stifle the Christmas spirit, as witnessed by these hordes of holiday shoppers crammed onto the main floor of Kern's Department Store, at Woodward and Gratiot. The emporium was marked by exquisite touches, such as marble floors, mahogany counters, and soaring ceilings. Kern's, founded in 1883 by German immigrant Ernst Kern, was originally on St. Antoine, and later moved to Randolph Street. The retailer continued to enlarge, and finally ended up at its Woodward location, which saw several building expansions throughout the years, the last of which was a 10-story addition in 1929. When Kern died in 1901, his sons Otto and Ernst Jr. ran the burgeoning company. Both brothers lived in the city's elegant Boston-Edison district. Otto's sons also became involved in management. Kern's remained a third-generation family business until 1957, when it was sold to the Buffalo, N.Y.-based Sattler's Inc. However, management changes and business problems led to the closing of Kern's on Dec. 23, 1959. Although the building was razed in the 1960s, one part of Kern's was salvaged, its famous clock, which was a downtown icon. Scores of Detroiters were heard to say, "I'll meet you under the Kern's clock." The landmark timepiece, which was refurbished by Compuware Corp., stands near its original site on Woodward, a constant reminder of Detroit's retailing past.

~❧~

1933 THESE BOOZE-SWILLING REVELERS, ALL *Detroit News* EMPLOYEES, ARE TOASTING THE repeal of Prohibition at Adams Restaurant in downtown Detroit. The 18th Amendment to the U.S. Constitution, which went into effect in 1920, forbade the selling, transportation, and consumption of alcohol, except for scientific or medicinal purposes. But Michigan had been dry even earlier; a state Prohibition law had been on the books since 1918. But the edict turned out to be all wet. Prohibition was a colossal failure, and nowhere was that more evident than in Detroit, where bootlegging was rampant. In fact, the Detroit-Windsor Tunnel was dubbed the Detroit-Windsor Funnel because of the steady flow of hooch from Canada. Belle Isle and Grosse Ile were favorite places for rumrunners, many of whom got rich. Ecorse was another conduit for illegal spirits. In Hamtramck, thirsty autoworkers could easily get a libation from "car bars" that dispensed drinks outside factories. Blind pigs thrived throughout the city, and the feds barely made a dent against the army of ingenious smugglers and defiant scofflaws. "Anyone who can't get a drink isn't trying" was a popular saying among Detroiters. Prohibition, which proponents said would reduce crime, had just the opposite effect. Organized crime was prevalent, marked by gang wars and murder. Finally, in 1933, it became legal again to imbibe.

1934

BETSY ROSS WOULD HAVE TO BE CLONED MANY TIMES OVER TO SEW THIS, THE world's largest flag, which was draped across the Woodward façade of the J.L. Hudson department store every June on Flag Day, as well as on other patriotic holidays. It was first unfurled on Armistice Day, 1923, and even made an appearance at the 1939 World's Fair. The flag was retired in 1949; the following year, it took 55 men to hang the new one. In 1960, to mark the admission of Alaska and Hawaii to statehood a year earlier, six seamstresses' services were required to add the two stars, which measured 6 feet high each. (The stripes were 8 feet wide.) A mile of rope held the flag in place. The giant flag was last displayed in 1976, to commemorate the nation's bicentennial. It was then donated to the Smithsonian Institution.

1935

DETROIT HAS PRODUCED SOME TITANIC ATHLETES, BUT PERHAPS NONE SO inextricably linked to the city than "The Brown Bomber," Joe Louis. Even though he was born in Alabama, Louis grew up on the east side of Detroit, and residents have always claimed him as a native son. Here, the young boxer and his new bride, Marva, greet a group of children at the Chestnut Community House. Of all Louis' bouts, the one in which he thrashed German pugilist Max Schmeling on the evening of June 22, 1938, at Yankee Stadium, was his most famous. It took Louis just over two minutes to pummel Schmeling. It was repayment for the German fighter's defeat of Louis two years before, but in many people's eyes, it was also a symbolic victory of democracy over fascism. The triumph ignited a celebration in Detroit's Black Bottom neighborhood. Louis, born Joe Louis Barrow in 1914, was the heavyweight boxing champ for a dozen years. To pay off his debts, the aging boxer came out of retirement in 1951, but was defeated by the young Rocky Marciano. Louis died 30 years later, but there are several Detroit monuments that keep his spirit alive. The downtown arena where the Red Wings play is named after him, and Robert Graham's "fist sculpture" at Woodward and Jefferson (technically called *Memorial to Joe Louis*) is a city landmark. There's also a lesser-known bronze sculpture of Louis in the lobby of Cobo Hall.

1935

Today, opera lovers in metro Detroit can satisfy their vocal fix by soaking up performances by Michigan Opera Theatre at the Detroit Opera House. But there was a time when we didn't have our own opera company. Fans yearning to hear *Aida* or *Faust* had to wait eagerly for the annual spring tours by New York's Metropolitan Opera. Even before the Met tours, there was "Opera Under the Stars" at Navin Field, which became Briggs Stadium, then Tiger Stadium. Here, a crowd enjoys an opera on June 8, 1935, at what was then Navin Field. In November, Frank Navin died, and Walter O. Briggs became the sole owner of the Tigers. He put his name on the stadium beginning with the 1938 season.

1935

TWO OF DETROIT'S SPORTS GIANTS SHARE A LIGHT MOMENT AS BOXER JOE LOUIS ("The Brown Bomber") makes a playful jab at Tigers first baseman Henry "Hammerin' Hank" Greenberg. The year 1935 was a golden one for the Tigers; under catcher/manager Mickey Cochrane, they won their first World Series, trouncing the Chicago Cubs, four games to two. Greenberg, who was named the American League's Most Valuable Player for that year, led the majors with 170 RBIs, and slammed 36 homers. Louis also had a stellar year, defeating such opponents as Primo Carnera (at Yankee Stadium), Max Baer, and Roscoe Toles. Further glory awaited him; from 1937-49, he reigned as World Heavyweight Champion.

 THERE ARE FEW MORE EXHILARATING OUTDOOR WINTER PLEASURES THAN sledding and tobogganing, and these hardy souls at Detroit's Rouge Park seem to be having a high old time coasting down a slide on a hill. Rouge Park, on the city's far west side, is Detroit's largest park; in fact, at nearly 1,200 acres, it's about 40-percent larger than New York's Central Park. The City of Detroit bought the expanse from several farmers for $1.3 million in the 1920s. Technically, it should be called River Rouge Park, named for the river that meanders through the area for more than two miles, but metro Detroiters simply refer to it as "Rouge Park." Home to an 18-hole golf course, three swimming pools (two of them Olympic-size), 14 baseball diamonds, 11 tennis courts, and other amenities, the park in 2009 added a large stone sculpture to its grounds, titled *Growing Together*, by artist Larry Halbert. Friends of Rouge Park, an organization devoted to protecting and improving the park, was formed in 2002.

1936

THROUGHOUT THE YEARS, DETROITERS HAVE LOVED FUN AND GAMES. AMUSEMENT parks once were as popular as watermelon in July; among them were Electric Park on East Jefferson; Eastwood Park, in what is now Eastpointe; Bob-lo, on the Detroit River; Edgewater Park, on the west side of Detroit; and Jefferson Beach, along Lake St. Clair in St. Clair Shores, where this photo was taken of thrill-seekers on a white-knuckled roller-coaster ride. Jefferson Beach, off Jefferson between Nine and Ten Mile roads, opened in 1927 and was a big draw for more than 30 years. "There was a kiddie land, carousel, pavilion, rides, boating, swimming, and a roller coaster that was one of the largest in the country," said Cynthia Bieniek, archivist and librarian at the St. Clair Shores Public Library. "There was also a ballroom with a floating dance floor, which was quite an attraction. During World War II, big bands played there," she said. Indeed, an undated ad touted an appearance by the Joe Haymes Orchestra. Another unusual feature was an oval-shaped Ferris wheel called "The Swooper." In 1955, a fire swept through the park, which started in the funhouse, Bieniek said. The park plied on, but its days were numbered. In 1959, Jefferson Beach closed and it was turned into a marina. Today, the area is known as Jefferson Beach Marina. Although the amusement park was razed, the dance hall was left standing. It was used as a storage facility, but it burned down in 1998, Bieniek said.

1936

THIS IDYLLIC SUMMER SCENE LOOKS LIKE SOME EXOTIC LOCALE, BUT IT'S ACTUALLY Detroit's Water Works Park, just off East Jefferson near Cadillac Boulevard. The area's initial purpose was both utilitarian and recreational. In 1879, a water-pumping station and standpipe (to equalize pressure) were built to supply drinking water to the city, but the 110 acres included a public park with picnic sites, tennis courts, swimming, and baseball diamonds. The grounds also were home to a library and greenhouse. The 185-foot-tall standpipe seen in the background was a hit with Detroiters and tourists who climbed the tower's winding staircase to the observation deck, which afforded breathtaking views of the city. A large water-powered floral clock at the park's entrance became another attraction. In 1912, the name was changed to Gladwin Park, which didn't stick with residents, who still called it Water Works Park. The growing city needed additional pumping stations, and the standpipe was effectively obsolete by 1893. It remained a popular draw, though, until 1945, when the City Council deemed it unsafe and closed it. It was razed in 1962. There are few vestiges of the park's glory days, save for the Beaux Arts-style Hurlbut Memorial Gate facing Jefferson. It was erected in 1894 to honor Chauncey Hurlbut, a long-serving president of the Board of Water Commissioners. The area does, however, retain its original function of serving water to the city. In 2003, a sprawling wastewater-treatment facility was completed.

1937

Born a slave in Missouri in 1864, the young botanist-to-be George Washington Carver couldn't have remotely imagined that his birthplace would become a national monument, nor that a replica of that log cabin would be built in Dearborn, Mich. But that's exactly what Henry Ford did at Greenfield Village, in Carver's honor. The men, very close in age, became friends later in life. This picture shows Carver addressing what is most likely the Chemurgic Conference, sponsored by Henry Ford, at the Dearborn Inn, circa 1937. Ford visited Carver at the Tuskegee Institute in Alabama, where Carver was a faculty member, and Carver came to see Ford at his nutrition lab as late as 1942. Ahead of their time, the two men discussed biofuel alternatives to gasoline, which they knew would one day be scarce. Carver, who died in 1943, was renowned for his experiments in finding multiple uses for peanuts, soybeans, and sweet potatoes, which included plastics, ink, shampoo, synthetic rubber, and paint. However, he didn't invent peanut butter, as is often claimed. The inventor was also an accomplished artist, and two of his paintings were exhibited at the 1893 World's Fair in Chicago. Carver was seldom without a flower in his buttonhole, seeing it as an opportunity to educate people about flora.

1937

FORD FIELD HAS BEEN THE DETROIT LIONS' HOME TURF SINCE 2002, BUT THE team has called several stadiums home through the years. From 1975 until the move downtown, the Lions played at the Pontiac Silverdome. Before that, the gridiron was at Briggs Stadium (later Tiger Stadium), starting in 1938. But the Lions' first den was the University of Detroit Stadium (also called Titan Stadium), where they played from 1934-37, and again in 1940. The stadium, which was at Six Mile Road near Fairfield in northwest Detroit, was the site of the team's first NFL Championship in 1935, when they trounced the New York Giants. Despite a strong start, attendance wasn't terrific in 1934, so team owner G.A. Richards decided to host a Thanksgiving Day game, which was broadcast nationally on the radio. The stadium sold out, thousands had to be turned away, and a holiday football tradition was born. In this shot, a band plays, presumably at halftime, in a Halloween Day game. U-D Titans football games were also held at the stadium until the school dropped the sport in the 1960s. Long a place of cheering and applause, the stadium fell silent in 1971, when it was razed.

1938

CHINESE-AMERICANS TAKE TO THE STREETS IN DETROIT TO PROTEST JAPANESE aggression in China during the Second Sino-Japanese War. The Japanese invaded Manchuria in 1931, but by 1937 full-fledged war broke out, and such major cities as Beijing, Nanjing, and Shanghai soon fell. The bloody conflict didn't end until the Japanese surrendered to the Allies in 1945. The exact location of this photo is unknown, although it was very likely around Third and Michigan, then the site of Detroit's Chinatown, which numbered around 3,000 people. After urban-renewal projects and the construction of the Lodge Freeway tore the old neighborhood asunder, many of Detroit's Chinese resettled in the vicinity of Cass and Peterboro in the early '60s. However, that enclave wasn't as large as the original Chinatown. Eventually, most of the Chinese residents left. Today, the Chinese-American population is scattered throughout metro Detroit, with the highest concentration in Oakland County.

1939

WITH "GREETINGS FROM DETROIT" PLASTERED ACROSS IT, THIS PHOTO COULD have made a great postcard. Packed with tourists (and maybe some locals), this new topless sightseeing bus rolls out for a day on the town. Then the nation's fourth-largest city, Detroit had a lot of sights to see in 1939: several auto factories; lavish residential neighborhoods such as Palmer Woods, Indian Village, and Boston-Edison; the Vernor's bottling plant; Belle Isle; Fort Wayne; Water Works Park; palatial downtown theaters like the Michigan, United Artists, Broadway-Capitol, and Fox; the GM Building (at the time the world's second-largest office building); the newly christened Briggs Stadium; the Cultural Center; Stroh's Brewery; a thriving downtown retail area; the Maccabees Building (where popular radio shows such as *The Lone Ranger* and *The Green Hornet* were broadcast from WXYZ's studio); three newspaper plants; scores of majestic churches and synagogues; and skyscrapers, including the Penobscot, then the city's tallest structure at 47 stories. After a tour of Detroit, these visitors no doubt had plenty to write home about.

1939

For almost 50 years, the 47-story Penobscot Building, at Griswold and Fort streets, reigned as Detroit's tallest structure. Here, a man and a woman perched on the observation deck take in an eagle's-eye view of the city. Built in 1928, the Art Deco skyscraper is distinguished by Native American motifs from the Penobscot tribe in Maine and an unusually dramatic design by architect Wirt Rowland. The first 30 stories are symmetrical, but the top 17 are marked by ever-narrowing setbacks and crowned by a bright-red neon ball. Rowland, then employed by the architectural firm Smith, Hinchman & Grylls, also designed Detroit's Buhl (1925) and Guardian (1929) buildings. The commanding granite-and-limestone tower was erected during Detroit's big building boom of the Roaring '20s, but the Penobscot actually has two older sections, built in 1905 and 1916. After the 73-story main tower of the Renaissance Center opened in 1977 (now GM's world headquarters), the Penobscot was knocked off its throne as Detroit's highest edifice. And when One Detroit Center opened in 1992, the Penobscot was bumped down to third tallest. But it remains one of the city's most regal buildings.

1939

September means back to school, but we're accustomed to seeing younger students than these in the classroom. The adults pictured here are attending "Americanization" night school at Detroit's Chadsey High School. They are most likely Polish immigrants, since the area around Chadsey, on Martin Street on the west side of Detroit, was at the time a heavily Polish neighborhood. "Americanization" involved teaching immigrants English, civics, and American culture. However, latter-day social critics held that, in an effort to assimilate immigrants, the classes (which were taught all over the country) stripped away too much of the immigrants' culture and ethnic identity. The school was named for Charles E. Chadsey, superintendent of Detroit schools from 1912-1919. Chadsey High opened on Columbus Day, 1931, which served as the inspiration to name its athletic teams The Explorers and its yearbook *The Compass*. Alas, Chadsey closed and was demolished in February 2011, along with the nearby Munger Middle School, to make way for a new pre-K-to-8 school.

1942 ANYONE WITH A SWEET TOOTH IS FAMILIAR WITH AWREY BAKERIES INC., which has been whipping up treats since 1910. Products such as Homestyle cinnamon rolls, Long John coffee cake, French buttercream cake, and glazed dunkers — all bearing the famous Awrey windmill logo on the label — have kept Detroiters on a sugar high for generations. Years ago, Awrey service stores were located within larger markets. In a 2005 interview, then Awrey Vice President Betty Jean Awrey said, "At one time, we had 2,000 salesladies wearing those crisp aprons and little white hats." She also recalled the popularity of the bakery's downtown store at Griswold and State. "Customers would wrap around the building waiting for hot-cross buns or lemon meringue pie. It was incredible in those days." In this photo, female employees are all smiles as they frost cakes in the old Awrey plant on Tireman, on Detroit's west side. In 1967, the company relocated to Livonia. In 2005, Awrey filed for Chapter 11 bankruptcy protection, and the family-owned operation was sold to Illinois-based Hilco Equity Management and New York-based Monomoy Capital Partners. But the good news is that the new owners kept the Awrey name and continue to make the yummy favorites.

1943

IN THE 1940s, FASHIONABLE AND ELEGANT DETROIT WOMEN HAD A BEVY OF high-end retailers where they could indulge their taste for haute couture. Uptown in the New Center area, there was Saks Fifth Avenue, at Second and Lothrop, and Julie, in the Fisher Building. Downtown, in addition to the department stores, there were such chic shops as Russeks, Himelhoch's, Kline's, Sax Kay, Milgrim, B. Siegel, and D.J. Healy. Healy's flagship store was on Woodward, just south of Grand Circus Park, but it also had several neighborhood shops, including this one at Jefferson and Chalmers, on Detroit's east side. According to Polk's 1938 *Detroit City Directory*, there were nine D.J. Healy locations: downtown Detroit, Dearborn, Highland Park, Birmingham, and five additional stores in the city — Six Mile and Gratiot; Grand River and Southfield; Cass at West Grand Boulevard; Six Mile and San Juan; and the East Jefferson location. Founded in the 1870s, D.J. Healy also sold fine art for several years. Like so many retailers that once defined Detroit, it has vanished from the shopping scene.

 THERE'S A LOT OF GROUSING TODAY ABOUT THE AREA'S LACK OF MASS TRANSIT, but in the 1940s there was little complaint. In fact, public transportation hummed, with Detroiters having their choice of taking streetcars, buses, or commuter trains to get around. This bus driver, photographed on Aug. 24, 1944, holds a transfer for a passenger. Advertisements were plastered inside and outside buses; the one in this shot touts Fox De Luxe Beer. The year 1945 saw the greatest ridership on streetcars and buses in Detroit history, but significant changes would soon affect how Detroiters commuted. The last streetcar rumbled down Woodward in 1956, and some blamed General Motors, which built Detroit's buses, for the demise of streetcars. Freeway construction during the '50s and '60s, combined with the exodus of Detroiters to the suburbs, further cemented the automobile's dominance.

 Sports championships have always brought out throngs of revelers to the city's streets. But few celebrations were as spontaneous and heartfelt as the crowds that jammed downtown Detroit when World War II ended. Although Germany had surrendered in May 1945, the Japanese didn't capitulate until Aug. 14. On that evening, an estimated 500,000 Detroiters spilled out into downtown thoroughfares, celebrating not only an end to the bloodshed, but years of rationing, air-raid siren warnings, practice blackouts, and other inconveniences. Detroit contributed mightily to the war effort. Factories that had made Packards, Hudsons, Fords, Chryslers, Chevrolets, and other cars shifted focus, cranking out tanks, planes, aircraft bombs, and Army trucks, earning the city the moniker "The Arsenal of Democracy." And more than 600,000 Michigan residents — about 200,000 of them Detroiters — served in the armed forces during World War II.

1945

THERE AREN'T MANY COMPANIES THAT CAN CROW ABOUT BEING IN BUSINESS for a century, never mind almost 140 years. But since opening its first store in downtown Detroit on June 17, 1875, Sanders has been satisfying our collective sweet tooth. Parlors soon began popping up all over town. In addition to sundaes, sodas, hot-fudge cream puffs, and "bumpy cake," Sanders added soups and sandwiches to its counter service. By the 1960s, there were 60 Sanders in metro Detroit, and the company also did a brisk business selling its goods in supermarkets. The little lad in this circa-1945 picture isn't going to let a height disadvantage deter him from getting to his soda as he kneels on his chair to give him a boost at the counter. Eventually, things turned sour for the purveyor of sweets, and the retail outlets shuttered by the 1990s, although toppings, cakes, and chocolates continued to be sold elsewhere. In 2002, Clinton Township-based Morley Brands bought and resuscitated Sanders. Within a few years, parlors serving sodas and sundaes returned to the landscape. Today, there are counters in Birmingham, Grosse Pointe, Rochester, Livonia, Wyandotte, Clinton Township, Eastpointe, and Novi, as well as seasonally on Mackinac Island. Recently, the Novi location, in Twelve Oaks Mall, also started serving lunches, something other counters will be doing "in the coming years," said Tiffany Van Hemm, director of public relations for Morley Candy/Sanders. She also said there are plans to open even more parlors.

1945 To get a bird's-eye view of the city, you don't necessarily have to be equipped with wings. Betty Fox, part of the aerialist/skydancing team of Benny and Betty Fox, fearlessly executes one of her famous "split jumps" high above downtown Detroit in this circa-1945 photo. It's difficult to see, but there's a platform under her, extending from the beam. The couple's perch (left) is the roof of the Fort Shelby Hotel (now the Doubletree Guest Suites Detroit Downtown — Fort Shelby). The thoroughfare below is Fort Street; the low building in the foreground is The Detroit Club. The Foxes took their lofty daredevil act to cities around the country, and the most exciting part occurred when they danced on an 18-inch-wide disc, culminating in the "death whirl," in which Betty would wrap her legs around Benny's waist and he'd rotate like a banshee, thrilling the heart-thumping crowd below.

Today, the word "projects," as it relates to housing, often carries a pejorative tone. But when many were built in the 1940s and '50s, they were places of pride for residents — and a welcome relief from the crammed dwellings they had previously called home. There were only about 6,000 African-Americans living in Detroit in 1910, but that number swelled to 120,000 by 1930, and grew steadily after that. Most lived in congested, older areas on the lower east side. In the late 1930s, the low-rise Brewster Homes, the nation's first federally funded housing project for blacks, opened. Situated in the area near Brewster Street and St. Antoine, they were built for the "working poor," and potential residents had to have proof of employment to live there. The vast majority of residents were African-American. This photograph shows a tidy Brewster playground (notice the woman in the background with a broom). In 1952, a cluster of six high-rise towers opened, and the conglomeration became known as the Brewster-Douglass Projects. Three young women who later became known as The Supremes met there in the '50s. In a 2005 interview with *Hour Detroit*, Supreme Mary Wilson spoke of her fond Brewster memories. The original low-rise homes were torn down in the '90s and replaced with townhouses, now called New Brewster Homes. Two of the high-rises also were razed since then.

1946

Despite the excitement surrounding GM's Volt, the electric car is nothing new. In the early 20th century, there were several companies manufacturing electrics, including Detroit Electric, Anthony Electric, Rauch & Lang, and Baker Motor Vehicle Co. Here, Charles Brady King (left), who designed and drove the first car to take to the streets of Detroit in 1896 (three months before Henry Ford), is perched next to Benson Ford Sr. in a vintage Cleveland-made Baker. The occasion was likely part of the Golden Automotive Jubilee, marking the 50th anniversary of the automobile in Detroit, which included a splashy parade and other events. Electrics were preferable to gasoline-powered autos for several reasons. There was no need for a crank, they were quiet, and they emitted no fumes. There was one major downside, though: Electrics were more expensive. Fans of electric cars included Thomas Edison (naturally) and Henry Ford's wife, Clara, who tooled around in a 1914 Detroit Electric Brougham until the 1930s. Comedian Jay Leno, a fervent car buff, owns a renovated 1909 Baker Electric Coupe. When the electric starter was introduced in 1912, obviating the need for a hand crank, cars that ran on gasoline became far more attractive. That invention, together with Henry Ford's affordable Model T (about half the price of an electric auto), pulled the plug on the electric car. But a surge of renewed interest amid spiking gas prices and zero-emission mandates could well mean that a car long thought of as quaint is ready to ride high again.

1914
FORD

BAKER ELECTRIC

The Edison Institute

1947

IN DOWNTOWN DETROIT DURING THE '40s, DAPPER GENTLEMEN HAD AN embarrassment of wardrobe riches to choose from. Emporiums catering to well-dressed males included Whaling's, J.M. Citron, S.L. Bird & Sons, Hughes & Hatcher, Kilgore and Hurd, Scholnick's, Capper & Capper, and Harry Suffrin — in addition to the department stores. The expansive Harry Suffrin shop, on Shelby Street, is shown here on a well-trafficked day. The store was founded in 1922 and became famous for customer service, which included free alterations. In the late 1950s, Harry Suffrin merged with Hughes & Hatcher to become Hughes-Hatcher-Suffrin, identifiable by its signature script on logos. Locations sprang up all over metro Detroit, but the company eventually went out of business in the 1980s.

1947 THROUGH THE YEARS, BELLE ISLE'S AMENITIES HAVE INCLUDED AN AQUARIUM, conservatory, canoes, skating pavilion, casino, and golf course, but for many Detroiters the one with the fondest association is the Belle Isle Children's Zoo, which opened in 1947. A sign on the building in this photo states that admission was 8 cents, plus 2 cents' tax. Visiting tykes ogled such cute creatures as baby elephants, and children were also permitted to feed and pet deer, goats, and other animals. In 1980, the Children's Zoo was renovated and larger animals were added. It was renamed the Belle Isle Safari Zoo, which later became known simply as the Belle Isle Zoo. It closed in 2004, but in the following year the Belle Isle Nature Zoo opened, home to European fallow deer that once roamed the island, an exhibit of native Michigan turtles, and an indoor beehive.

1948 Briggs Stadium (renamed Tiger Stadium in 1961) was the last ballpark in the American League to add night games. Team owner Walter Briggs was a traditionalist and believed baseball should be played in daylight, but he finally relented and eight light towers were affixed to the stadium. This aerial view documents the Tigers' first night game on June 15, 1948. Apparently, Detroiters liked being night-owl fans; a crowd of 54,480 showed up that evening to see the Bengals trounce Philadelphia, 4-1. The Tiger roster that year included Dizzy Trout, Virgil Trucks, Eddie Mayo, and third baseman George Kell, who, beginning in 1957, launched a long career as a play-by-play announcer, with most of those years spent calling games for the Tigers in his signature Arkansas drawl.

❧

1949

IF IT HAPPENED TO SNOW DURING THE OLD J.L. HUDSON THANKSGIVING Day Parade, the wintry weather just seemed to add to the festive mood. In 1949, snowflakes heightened the holiday spirit, as evidenced by the jolly fellow in red from his perch in front of Hudson's, waving to throngs of people crammed on Woodward Avenue. His trusty reindeer are in the foreground. The parade always ended in front of Hudson's with Santa Claus greeting the crowd, which officially signaled the start of the holiday retail season. Back in '49, downtown Detroit was incontestably the area's shopping mecca, but the sprouting of suburban shopping malls was on the horizon. Five years later, Northland opened, followed in three years by Eastland, drawing scores of shoppers away from the downtown hub.

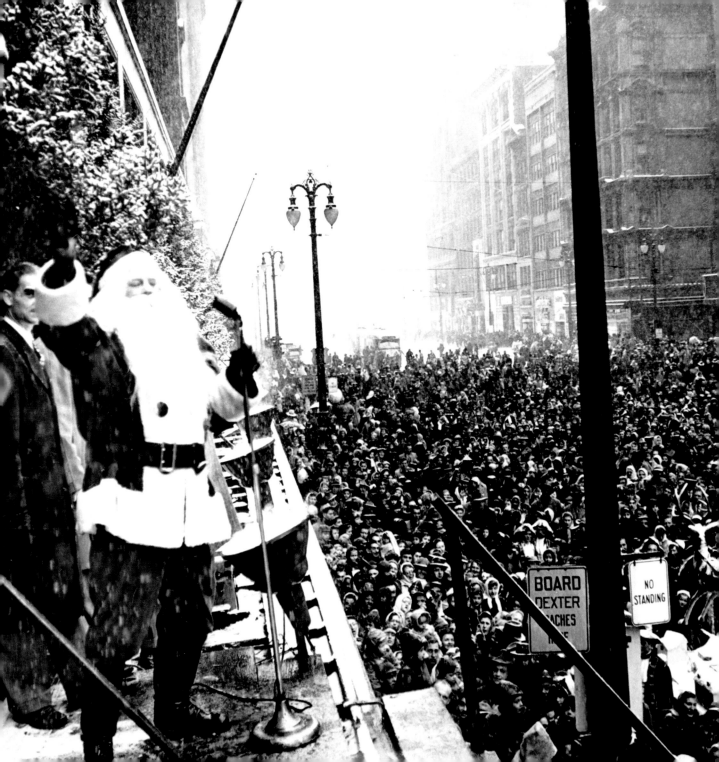

1952 "I like Ike" was the campaign slogan of Dwight D. Eisenhower (nicknamed Ike) and, judging by this downtown crowd on Woodward Avenue in front of Hudson's, many Detroiters concurred, as the Republican presidential candidate waves with both hands to the masses. A World War II hero, Eisenhower cruised to victory in November over his opponent, Illinois Gov. Adlai Stevenson II who, despite his coruscating wit and gift for oratory, was deemed by many Americans to be too much of an egghead. Eisenhower's triumph ended 20 years of Democratic control of the White House. On this sunny afternoon (Flag Day, June 14) Eisenhower delivered a speech in front of Old City Hall. Michigan was a red state in '52, with Eisenhower garnering more votes than Stevenson. In 1956, Ike ran for a second term, trouncing Stevenson more soundly than in '52, and Michigan again went Republican. Eisenhower died in 1969.

1953 THE SHUBERT THEATRE, AT THE CORNER OF SHELBY AND LAFAYETTE IN downtown Detroit, was a longtime venue for legitimate theater. Here, the marquee is touting Janet Blair and Webb Tilton in Rodgers and Hammerstein's *South Pacific*. Along with the Cass Theatre, across the street on Lafayette, the Shubert hosted many productions that either were bound for Broadway or had already been on the Great White Way. The theater, originally named the Orpheum, opened in 1914 as a vaudeville house. In 1925, it was renamed the Shubert Lafayette, redubbed the Lafayette in the '30s, reverted to the Shubert Lafayette in the '40s, before ultimately being called simply the Shubert, in 1952. To further confuse matters, there was, from 1919 to 1931, a Shubert Detroit theater at the original Detroit Opera House on Campus Martius. The Nederlanders managed the Shubert, but abandoned it when their Broadway showcase moved to the remodeled Fisher Theatre in the early '60s. Sadly, the lovely old Italianate theater on Lafayette, which included interior murals by Maxfield Parrish, was razed in 1964.

1954

GRAND CIRCUS PARK, ON THE NORTHERN EDGE OF DOWNTOWN AT WOODWARD and Adams, for many years served as a serene gateway to the city's central business district. In the 19th century, mansions surrounded the park, but the boom years of the next century saw skyscrapers replacing the homes. These men are taking a rest from the hubbub of the city on Oct. 4, 1954. They're clustered around a statue/fountain dedicated to Russell A. Alger (1836-1907), who served as Michigan governor, U.S. senator, and secretary of war in President McKinley's cabinet. Alger was also a prominent lumber baron and Civil War hero. His son built the elegant Russell A. Alger home on Lake Shore Drive in Grosse Pointe Farms, which today serves as the Grosse Pointe War Memorial. Although there's a plaque dedicated to Alger on the monument's base (not visible), the statue is of a laurel-crowned woman, symbolizing the state of Michigan. One hand is extended in greeting, while the other grasps a sword and shield emblazoned with the state's great seal. On the pedestal, water gushes from the mouths of two lions. The monument, designed by Daniel Chester French — who also created the sculpture of Abraham Lincoln at the Lincoln Memorial and the Concord Minute Man in Concord, Mass. — was unveiled in 1921. In the background stands the old Hotel Tuller, which was torn down in the 1980s.

1955

In today's concrete jungles, a 10-story building seems puny. But when the Hammond Building was erected in 1890 at Fort and Griswold at a cost of $750,000, it was Detroit's first skyscraper and one of the world's largest masonry structures. The building was named after George H. Hammond, who was in the meatpacking industry. He made his fortune by buying the patent for the refrigerated boxcar in 1869, an invention of Detroit fish merchant William Davis. Structural steel and elevators made skyscrapers possible in the late 19th century, but some skittish Detroiters initially refused to venture into the Hammond, fearing for their safety because the building might collapse. More adventuresome souls couldn't wait to ascend to the roof for a bird's-eye view. To mark the grand opening, an acrobat strode a cable linking the Hammond to City Hall (left foreground). The Hammond's day in the sun was brief, though, as larger downtown structures such as the Majestic, Ford, and Dime buildings soon went up, dwarfing the Hammond. By the time this photo was taken, the Hammond Building's days were numbered. It was razed to accommodate the new headquarters of the National Bank of Detroit (later renamed Bank One and now the Chase Tower), which opened in 1959.

1957

FEW THINGS IN THE AUTO INDUSTRY ARE MORE EXCITING THAN THE LAUNCHING of a new model. When Ford Motor Co.'s Edsel — named after the son of company founder Henry Ford — was introduced, it received a splashy debut. In this photo taken in Dearborn, Edsel Ford's sons (left to right: William Clay Ford, Benson Ford Sr., and Henry Ford II) sit in a 1958 Citation two-door convertible. Edsel Ford had been president of the Ford Motor Co. from 1919 until his death in 1943. After months of hype and an extensive ad campaign, the Edsel was unveiled to the public in September 1957. But the Edsel's star fell as swiftly as it had risen. Sluggish sales were partly attributable to an economic recession, but there also were production woes, and some models left the assembly line with missing parts. In addition, several critics ridiculed the car's design, particularly the awkward-looking grille. Soon the Edsel became synonymous with the word lemon, and the car lasted only three model years: 1958, '59 and '60. But today, the Edsel has garnered some respect. There are two organizations devoted to the preservation of the car — the Edsel Owners Club and the International Edsel Club. In a 2005 interview, Dennis Majors of Monroe, the state coordinator of both clubs and the owner of seven Edsels, acknowledged that "quality control was not the strong point at Ford then," but says the car's design got a bum rap. "If you put the Edsel side by side with a Buick or Oldsmobile from that time, the Edsel is a much cleaner-designed car. And the taillights were higher, so they could be seen in traffic, which was better for safety concerns."

1957

THE HULKING OLYMPIA STADIUM, NICKNAMED "THE OLD RED BARN" BECAUSE of its red-brick exterior, will be linked forever with the Detroit Red Wings, but it was home to many kinds of events. When Olympia opened in October 1927, at Grand River and McGraw, the first presentation was a rodeo. Before their 1961 move to Cobo, the Pistons played hoops there. Boxing drew huge crowds to Olympia. Jake LaMotta and Sugar Ray Robinson duked it out in the '40s. A young Joe Louis climbed into the ring in 1934. The Beatles played there twice — in 1964 and 1966 — to thousands of screaming fans. Elvis Presley, Cream, and Elton John rocked the rafters, too. Wrestling was another attraction at Olympia, as were political rallies, the Ice Follies, even roller derbies. But hockey ruled at Olympia. Though it was cavernous, the interior was nevertheless intimate, and fans reveled in seeing such icons as Gordie Howe, Terry Sawchuck, and Ted Lindsay up close. In this photograph, the ice is resurfaced between periods at a 1957 game. It was a golden decade for the Wings; they won four Stanley Cups in the '50s. The Red Wings skated for the last time at Olympia in 1979, before moving to Joe Louis Arena. Along with a million memories, Olympia came crashing down in 1986.

1957

WITH ALL THEIR BRICKS, MORTAR, GRIME, AND CONCRETE, CITIES CAN LOOK pretty bleak, but flowers always brighten up an urban landscape, as this colorful floral clock in front of Old City Hall did. Although the building was capped by a clock tower, the ground-level timepiece was a refreshing sight during warm weather. These city workers tend to the clock, studded with intricately arranged flowers, on a late-spring day. In an earlier era, floral clocks were all the rage; there was one at the entrance to Water Works Park on East Jefferson as well. It became such a popular Detroit symbol that it appeared on postcards. That clock was moved to Greenfield Village in 1934 and was on view there from 1935 to 1974. Old City Hall, a stately Renaissance Revival marvel decorated with sculptures carved by Julius Melchers, was an even greater Detroit emblem. Dedicated in 1871, it stood for 90 years near what is now Kennedy Square. Despite an outcry from preservationists, it was razed in 1961.

1957

THIS IMAGE OF EASTGATE CENTER, AT GRATIOT AND FRAZHO IN ROSEVILLE, crystallizes many social and cultural facets of the 1950s, both locally and nationally. Several once-prominent Detroit-area businesses are pictured: Federal Department Store, Wrigley's supermarket, and S.S. Kresge Co. — all vanished today. The design of the signage, with the modified atomic energy symbol, virtually screams 1950s. The photo also suggests the urban sprawl of that decade. New homes were springing up in the suburbs of America, and metro Detroit was a prime example. After reaching an apex of nearly 2 million residents in 1950, the city proper lost almost 180,000 people a decade later. On the east side, Roseville, East Detroit (now Eastpointe), Harper Woods, and St. Clair Shores experienced a population boom. In a 2007 interview, Jackie Saturley of the Roseville Public Library said the Federal store in this photo opened in 1954, but the entire shopping center debuted in 1955, with a grand opening featuring Clarabell the Clown, Chief Thunderthud, and other *Howdy Doody Show* characters, as well as Lee Meriwether, Miss America of 1955. A new Buick was raffled off, too. Saturley added that the area where Eastgate stands was formerly Packard Field, later known as Hartung Airport and Gratiot Airport.

1961 THE MERCURY THEATRE, AT SIX MILE AND SCHAEFER IN NORTHWEST DETROIT, was one of the city's most unusual neighborhood theaters. Built in 1941, the building's architecture was Art Moderne in style, and astronomical-themed murals (in keeping with the planetary name) adorned the interior. The 2,000-seat theater was also among the first outside the downtown palaces that showed first-run films. In a 2001 interview with *Hour Detroit*, Hollywood producer and native Detroiter Jerry Bruckheimer fondly recalled watching Saturday matinees at the Mercury. At the top of the sign, notice the winged motif, a reference to Mercury, messenger to the gods, who had wings affixed to his feet. On the marquee is *Exodus*, Otto Preminger's epic flick starring Paul Newman and Eva Marie Saint. Mercury was also the god of commerce, appropriate considering that the theater was clustered in a shopping area, which in this shot included Wrigley's and A&P supermarkets, as well as F.W. Woolworth, once very familiar retail names. Like many large old theaters, the Mercury eventually hit hard times. In 1985, it was "twinned" and renamed the Metro Mercury I & II, but the theater still struggled. It was razed in the late '90s.

1961 BEGINNING IN THE 1950S, MALLS BECAME RETAIL MAGNETS FOR THE GROWING suburban population. Northland, in Southfield, opened in 1954, followed by Eastland, in Harper Woods, which started business on July 26, 1957. Both were anchored by J.L. Hudson's and built near freeways (the Lodge for Northland and the soon-to-open I-94 for Eastland), as a convenience for the increasingly car-dependent populace. Here, an "Easter Parade" fashion show crowds Eastland, at Eight Mile and Kelly. Eastland is distinguished by two sculptures, which appeal particularly to children: Marshall M. Fredericks' *The Lion and the Mouse* and William McVey's *The Hippo*. Originally, Eastland Center wasn't enclosed; that happened in 1975. Those with long memories will recall some of Eastland's first stores: Hudson's, Hughes & Hatcher, Cunningham Drug Store, Stouffer's restaurant, S.S. Kresge, Morley's Candies, Sanders, Baker's Shoes, Alexander & Hornung, and Robinson Furniture Co.

1961 Movie fans queue up at the Madison Theatre on Witherell Street in downtown Detroit for a preview screening of *Splendor in the Grass*, starring Warren Beatty and Natalie Wood. Built in 1917, the Madison was neoclassical in style and less ostentatious than other downtown movie palaces that followed in the '20s. It was designed by C. Howard Crane, who was also responsible for the Adams, Fox, Capitol (now the Detroit Opera House), Orchestra Hall, and other theaters. The Madison had the distinction of showing the first talking movie in Detroit: *The Jazz Singer*, which opened on Christmas Day, 1927. This photo shows a spiffed-up Madison, because in 1961 the theater was renovated, complete with a new marquee. In the 1950s and '60s, the Madison survived by booking several long-running films, such as *The Ten Commandments* and *Spartacus*, said Mike Hauser, co-author of *Detroit's Downtown Movie Palaces* (Arcadia Publishing). "It was a tough time in the movie business with television growing," Hauser said. "But the Madison had long runs with several films, including a 68-week run of *The Sound of Music*." However, grim days lay ahead, and horror films became common fare. Appropriately, the Madison's final film was *The Dead Zone*, in 1983. In 2001, the 1,800-seat auditorium was demolished, but the office portion of the structure was left standing. Quicken Loans, Inc. bought the building in 2011.

1963

BEFORE THEY MADE THEIR SMASH APPEARANCES ON BROADWAY, SEVERAL shows opened first in Detroit at the Fisher Theatre. In late 1963, *Hello, Dolly!* premiered in Detroit with Carol Channing as the lovable matchmaker, Dolly Gallagher Levi. Jerry Herman's high-kicking title tune, along with "Before the Parade Passes" and "It Only Takes a Moment," propelled the musical into one of the longest-running hits on Broadway. It opened in New York on Jan. 16, 1964. Here, Carol Channing exits the Fisher's stage door, presumably after a rehearsal or performance, in November of 1963. The show became Channing's signature role, although Ethel Merman rejected the part before her. The Fisher was originally a Mayan-themed movie palace, but after a modernization by the Nederlander organization in 1961, it reopened as a legitimate theater. In 1964, another infectious musical premiered at the Fisher before its storied Broadway run: *Fiddler on the Roof.*

1964

BEFORE THERE WAS A VACCINE FOR PARALYTIC POLIO, THE FEAR OF CONTRACTING it gripped the nation for much of the 20th century. In 1921, future president Franklin Delano Roosevelt was diagnosed with the disease at 39, leaving him paralyzed from the waist down. The peak year in 1952 witnessed almost 58,000 cases of polio in the United States, 21,000 of them the paralytic type. At its most severe, the disease atrophied breathing muscles, and patients, many of whom were schoolchildren, were placed in "iron lungs." Others suffered damage to their limbs, necessitating crutches. The contagious disease, spread through stool and saliva, so terrified people that, even on scorching days, public swimming pools and beaches were nearly empty. Dr. Jonas Salk devised the first vaccine (IPV, or inactivated poliovirus vaccine), delivered by injection, in 1955. Then, in 1961, Dr. Albert Sabin created the OPV, or oral poliovirus vaccine, which was a weakened live vaccine. This snaking line of people at the old Herman Kiefer Hospital in Detroit — now the Herman Kiefer Health Complex — wait for oral vaccines, which, in 1964, was the recommended treatment. Today, paralytic polio has been nearly eradicated, although the World Health Organization says the virus is still circulating in parts of Africa and Asia.

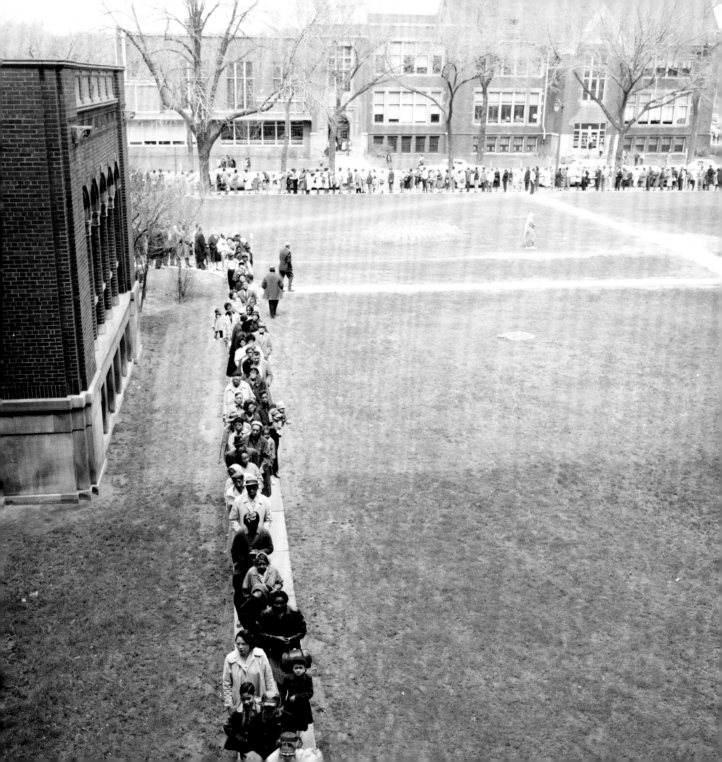

1964

IDEALLY, LIBRARIES ARE BUILT TO BE TEMPLES OF LEARNING, BUT MANY ARE also houses of great art. The Main Detroit Public Library, on Woodward in the Cultural Center, is exactly such a place. Designed by Cass Gilbert in 1921, the coolly elegant Italian Renaissance exterior is composed of limestone and white Vermont marble. But the interior is equally magnificent. In Adam Strohm Hall on the third floor, for instance, there's a triptych of murals on the west wall by John Stephens Coppin called *Man's Mobility* (pictured), a homage to the progression of transportation, completed in 1964. The middle panel depicts transportation in the present time, as a man, his eyes lifted heavenward, gazes transfixed as rockets ascend. Although born in Mitchell, Ontario, in 1904, Coppin was trained in Detroit and lived in the area for many decades. He died in 1986. Directly across from the triptych are three murals centering on early Detroit history, painted in 1921 by Detroit-born artist Gari Melchers. Still more murals, by American artist Edwin Howland Blashfield, are to be found on the third-floor stairwell. His five panels, completed in 1922, are devoted to the arts. In addition, throughout Adam Strohm Hall are stained-glass windows depicting the signs of the zodiac and the Muses, executed by Frederick J. Wiley, in 1921.

 It looks as if then Michigan Gov. George Romney is about to break into "Stop! In the Name of Love" with The Supremes, but he was likely on the band shell stage of the Michigan State Fair simply to introduce the Motown group, who were on a hit-making streak in 1965, releasing such chart-topping singles as "Back in My Arms Again," "Nothing but Heartaches," and, of course, "Stop! In the Name of Love." The State Fair attracted some of the biggest names in entertainment, and nabbing the hometown girls — Florence Ballard, Mary Wilson, and Diana Ross — to perform at the crest of their popularity was quite a coup. The group started in 1959 as a quartet called the Primettes, but they didn't have their first No. 1 hit until 1964 with "Where Did Our Love Go?" The Michigan State Fair was known as the nation's oldest; it began in 1849, and was held at the State Fairgrounds, on Woodward between State Fair Avenue and Eight Mile Road, since 1905. The event was an end-of-summer ritual for generations of Michiganians. However, state budget cuts, dwindling sponsors, and tepid attendance ended the fair's long run after the 2009 season.

1965

When, in 1959, Berry Gordy Jr. borrowed $800 from his family to start a record label, they knew it was a risky venture. After all, the 30-year-old Detroiter's résumé wasn't exactly overflowing with successes. He had a modest but brief career as a boxer. Then, in 1953, Gordy opened a record store that shuttered two years later. After that flop, he worked on the Lincoln-Mercury assembly line. But the $800 would turn out to be a phenomenally savvy investment. With it, Gordy founded Motown Records, originally called Tamla, in a two-story house on West Grand Boulevard. By 1960, Barrett Strong's "Money" charted as a hit. The next year, the Miracles' "Shop Around" became a million-seller, and the Marvelettes' "Please Mr. Postman" rocketed to No. 1. The former boxer would never be on the ropes again. Gordy, a songwriter himself, had a jeweler's eye for spotting gems. He hired only the best entertainers, writers, and arrangers. He was a shrewd businessman to boot. In this shot, he's surrounded by record albums of his star performers. The small studio on Grand Boulevard remained in use — it's The Motown Museum today — but Motown's business offices moved to a large building on Woodward. In 1972, Motown relocated to Los Angeles. However, "the Motown sound" will be linked forever with the city in which it was born.

 ANYONE WHO WANTS TO SEE THE METROPOLITAN OPERA PERFORM LIVE these days has to go to Lincoln Center in New York City. However, there was a time when the Met, like a cultural missionary, set out on tour and brought opera — and its most glittering stars — to several cities, including Minneapolis, Atlanta, Cleveland, Memphis, and Detroit. From 1959 to 1985, the Met performed a week's worth of operas in late May at Masonic Temple. Opening night was Monday, and two performances a (matinee and an evening show) concluded the run on Saturday. Opera lovers got to hear such celebrated singers as Franco Corelli, Leontyne Price, Joan Sutherland, Jon Vickers, Richard Tucker, Anna Moffo, Plácido Domingo, Nicolai Gedda, and Birgit Nilsson. The week was a glamorous affair, with Detroiters dressing to the nines. They gazed at lavishly attired socialites, who were often dropped off in limos and ascended the Masonic's steps, which were covered in red carpet. That's what's happening in this shot, as a fur-draped woman and her escort, bedecked in top hat and tails, climb the steps while onlookers peer. On this particular evening, Monday, May 24, 1965, opera week was getting started with a performance of Gian Carlo Menotti's *The Last Savage*, starring Roberta Peters and Teresa Stratas. The prohibitive cost of a traveling opera troupe eventually spelled the end of the Met tour, and on May 25, 1985, after a performance of *Rigoletto*, with Aldo Protti, Judith Blegen, and Detroit's own Ara Berberian, Detroiters bade a sad "addio" to the Met in Detroit.

1966

IF IT HADN'T HAD A MARQUEE, THE PUNCH AND JUDY WOULDN'T EVEN resemble a movie theater. Blending in demurely with the Colonial style shared by a stretch of businesses on Kercheval in Grosse Pointe Farms, the theater even had shutters on its windows. But then "the Punch," as locals called it, was a different breed of theater. In a time of ostentatious movie palaces seating several thousand, the Punch and Judy — named for the puppet-show characters — opened in 1930, revealing an understatedly elegant interior with only 600 seats (later expanded to 740 when the orchestra pit was appropriated for seating). A distinguishing feature was the smoking loge, which made it the only movie theater in Michigan where it was legal to light up. It also had its own tune. On opening night, the organist played "The Punch and Judy March" on the Wurlitzer, which was written expressly for the occasion. Architecturally, the Punch and Judy was a kissing cousin to the theater in Dearborn's Henry Ford Museum, which isn't surprising, considering that Robert O. Derrick designed both — and in the same year. The Punch was still going strong in 1966, evidenced by this queue of patrons snaking down Kercheval. But by the late '70s, attendance had ebbed, and the theater closed. It soon had a rebirth with midnight screenings of *The Rocky Horror Picture Show* and live performances by new-wavers Devo, the Ramones, and Patti Smith. By the early '80s, classic and art films graced the screen, but the lights dimmed for good in 1984. The theater was gutted, and the structure reopened in 1987 for office/retail use.

~&~

1966

CHRISTMAS ALWAYS SEEMS MORE FESTIVE AT NIGHT, WHEN TWINKLING lights and shimmering trees add drama and brilliance to the evening. During Detroit Aglow, downtown retailers and other businesses light up their seasonal displays, unofficially kicking off the holiday shopping season. In the '60s, the City of Detroit did its part in brightening the night by adding luster with decorations festooned on lampposts, as seen here on Fort Street. Another part of Detroit Aglow is the city's tree-lighting ceremony, officiated by the mayor, a tradition that continues to this day. The practice was begun by Mayor Albert Cobo in 1954. This photo also recalls the names of once-famous banking institutions now almost faded from memory: Bank of the Commonwealth and City National Bank.

~ ❧ ~

1966

No one even remotely familiar with Detroit's musical history can dismiss the importance of the Grande Ballroom, a virtual temple of rock 'n' roll. Not only did local bands perform there — the MC5 was considered its house band — but big-name performers such as Led Zeppelin, the Who, Cream, Big Brother & the Holding Company, the Grateful Dead, and the Yardbirds also rocked the rafters. But the Grande's (pronounced Grand-ee) beginnings were tentative. Attendance was sparse on Oct. 7, 1966, when it opened as a rock venue with the MC5 and The Chosen Few on the bill. The funky lettering on the poster seen in this opening-night photo was the work of Gary Grimshaw, whose posters and handbills became highly collectible. Word spread among metro Detroit youth, and the Grande, on Detroit's west side, at Grand River and Beverly (a block south of Joy), eventually was packed. Young people thought nothing of climbing the staircase to the second floor, where the expansive wooden dance floor and stage were. The Grande was the brainchild of Russ Gibb, a Dearborn schoolteacher and DJ, who was inspired by a visit to San Francisco's Fillmore Auditorium. The Grande's history stretches back to 1928, when it was built by Charles Agree, in a Moroccan-Spanish style. Agree also designed the Vanity Ballroom on Detroit's east side, the Hollywood Theatre on Fort Street, the Whittier Hotel off East Jefferson, and the Belcrest Apartments on Cass. In the 1940s, the Grande was a bastion for swing music. As a rock palace, the Grande's coda came on New Year's Eve, 1972, after which it was left to deteriorate.

1967

IT MAY NOT BE POSSIBLE TO WALK ON WATER, BUT IN THE 1960s PEOPLE were able to drive on water, provided they were behind the wheel of an Amphicar, the amphibious German-made vehicle built between 1961 and 1968. For these commuters tooling along the Detroit River, cruising on water certainly beat battling rush-hour traffic on land. The Amphicar could go in excess of 70 mph on land and, depending on the current, up to 10 mph on water. Interestingly, owners had to have two licenses — one for land and the other for water. All Amphicars were convertibles, with high rear fins and a four-cylinder engine in the rear. On water, they operated with nylon propellers, and the front wheels acted as rudders. Although amphibious vehicles were in use well before the '60s, particularly during World War II, the Amphicar was the first non-military one produced commercially. Its novelty, however, was short-lived. But Gibbs Technologies introduced its amphibious vehicle, the Aquada, to the U.S. market in 2009, and says it can exceed 30 mph on water.

FORMER DETROIT MAYOR COLEMAN A. YOUNG, FAMOUS FOR HIS FIERY TEMPER and salty tongue, may not have been everyone's idea of Santa Claus, but here he is on Dec. 22, 1974, as the jolly man in red, surrounded by children at the Manoogian Mansion. Young served longer than any other Detroit mayor — five terms — from 1974-94. The first black mayor of Motown, Democrat Young was elected in a close race over police chief John Nichols in 1973. Young was a state senator before becoming mayor and served in the all-black Tuskegee Airmen during World War II, when troops were segregated. Born in Tuscaloosa, Ala., in 1918, Young moved with his family to Detroit when he was 5. He died in 1997 of complications from emphysema at Detroit's Sinai Hospital.

1975

FOR MUCH OF THE 20TH CENTURY, IMMIGRANTS WERE ENCOURAGED TO become acclimated to American culture. Speaking a foreign tongue was frowned on. Even "ethnic" sounding names were shortened or otherwise changed. But by the 1970s, the tide had turned. Acknowledging one's heritage was something to be celebrated, not shunned. It was during that decade that the City of Detroit began to host summer-long ethnic festivals each weekend on the riverfront. Food, music, dancing, and other entertainment contributed to the festivities. Here, a mariachi band and dancer get into the spirit of things at the Mexican Festival. Most Mexican immigrants settled on Detroit's southwest side, and that enclave continues to have a large Latino population, earning it the nickname Mexicantown. Pontiac, Dearborn, and some Downriver communities also have sizable Mexican-American populations.

~∾~

1977

EACH SUMMER FOR MORE THAN 20 YEARS, THE TERRACE OF THE HOTEL Pontchartrain in downtown Detroit was filled with the strains of sweet music during its celebrated P'Jazz series. Some of the top names in jazz played at the Pontch from 1972 until 1994, including pianist and bandleader Count Basie, seen here in August of 1977 cutting a 400-pound birthday cake in the shape of a grand piano. The cake is inscribed: "Happy 73rd, Count. From your P'Jazz fans." Basie, whose real first name was William, died at the age of 80 in 1984. "The major acts that came here were phenomenal — Tony Bennett, the Glenn Miller Orchestra, Nancy Wilson, and so many others. It was unbelievable," said Lisa McFarland, then the hotel's sales and marketing director, in a 2005 interview. The hotel had a jazz pedigree that predated P'Jazz. In the 1960s, the Cabaret La Bohème (later known as the Top of the Pontch) was home to nightly jazz. Both local and national acts played on the 25th floor amid a décor inspired by French artist Toulouse-Lautrec. In 2003, P'Jazz resumed briefly. The Pontch, built in 1965, was renamed the Crowne Plaza Hotel Pontchartrain Detroit, then became the Detroit Riverside Hotel. It closed in August 2009.

~ ✦ ~

1979

ACTOR ED ASNER APPEARS TO BE MAKING HIMSELF AT HOME IN THIS *Detroit News* office, looking every bit the part of a hard-boiled journalist. It's no wonder, considering he played a gruff city editor at the time on the popular CBS drama *Lou Grant*, which aired from 1977 to 1982. Previously, Asner portrayed an irascible TV news producer on *The Mary Tyler Moore Show* (1970-77). Ben Burns, who in 1979 was assistant managing editor at *The News*, said Asner was in town to speak at the old Detroit Press Club downtown on Howard Street, and also toured the nearby *Detroit News* building. Burns later became the paper's executive editor and is now director of the journalism program at Wayne State University. In a 2009 interview, Burns said Asner was genuinely interested in journalism and possessed some of the traits of a classic newspaperman. "He was crusty and funny and reminded me of many editors I had known," Burns said. "He had opinions, too, and he made them known." But Burns added that Asner was also sociable and down to earth. "He was the kind of guy you'd like to go out with for a beer," he said.

1980

DETROIT PUT ON A GRAND OLD PARTY WHEN IT HOSTED THE REPUBLICAN National Convention more than three decades ago. From July 14 until July 17, 1980, Joe Louis Arena was packed with party loyalists, including such celebrities as Frank Sinatra and Elizabeth Taylor. Delegates nominated Ronald Reagan for president and George Herbert Walker Bush as vice president. Here, Reagan and future First Lady Nancy bask in the crowd's adulation. The convention had its dramatic moments because of the mystery surrounding the vice-presidential selection, which Reagan didn't announce until the convention's final day. Former President Gerald Ford was entertaining the possibility of accepting the number-two position, but he had certain stipulations about whom he wanted in cabinet posts. Disappointed, Reagan settled on Bush, who learned of his selection late in the evening of July 16. Bush was in his suite at the Hotel Pontchartrain when Reagan called him with the good news. (Reagan was staying at what was then the Westin Hotel in the Renaissance Center.) In his acceptance speech, Reagan thanked Detroit for its "warm hospitality." The Reagan-Bush ticket went on to trounce incumbent President Jimmy Carter in November, with independent John Anderson placing a distant third. Reagan and Bush were re-elected in 1984, and Bush himself became president in 1988.

Index

Index

Photography Credits